52-WEEK

ATTITUDE

of

GRATITUDE

JOURNAL

Elaine Zelker

This book is dedicated to YOU.
Know that someone out there knows you've got what it takes to
crush your goals and become the one you were meant to be.

I AM your biggest cheerleader.
I AM rooting for you.
I AM proud of you.
I AM confident you can win.
I AM on your side.

Now, it's your turn to believe the same!

What are you grateful for today?

Just look around...we have plenty to be grateful for.

Our family, our job, our car, neighbors, friends, the clouds, coffee in the morning, a warm house in winter, food in abundance in the refrigerator, clean water, comfortable shoes, the rain, the sun, the wind, electricity, sight, love...the list could go on and on...

Being grateful, scientifically, is also good for your health! In a 2013 study (1), findings suggest that grateful individuals experience better physical health, in part, because of their greater psychological health, propensity for healthy activities, and willingness to seek help for health concerns. This was especially true in older adults (over 50).

In 2015, Psychology Today states 7 Scientifically Proven Benefits of Gratitude (2):

> Gratitude opens the door to more relationships.
> Gratitude improves physical health.
> Gratitude improves psychological health.
> Gratitude enhances empathy and reduces aggression.
> Grateful people sleep better.
> Gratitude improves self-esteem
> Gratitude increases mental strength.

So basically, having an "attitude of gratitude" will not only make you a better person on the outside, it works wonders on the inside... literally!

In addition to having an attitude of gratitude, you have to believe in the magnitude of the 2 most powerful words in our language: I AM. For what comes after those two little words will shape you and give you the power to overcome anything. If you believe, you will become.

Why?

Because thoughts are powerful. Thoughts lead to action. Action overtime become habits and habits lead to long-lasting results.

Be grateful and believe in YOU.
Happy journaling.

1.   Hill PL, Allemand M, Roberts BW. (2013) Examining the pathways between gratitude and self-rated physical health across adulthood. Personality and Individual Differences https://www.ncbi.nlm.nih.gov/pubmed/23139438),
2.   Morin, Amy. "7 Scientifically Proven Benefits of Gratitude."
www.psychologytoday.com/us/blog/what-mentally-strong-people-dont-do/201504/7-scientifically-proven-benefits-gratitude.

Today I am grateful for:

SUNDAY

MONDAY

TUESDAY

WEDNESDAY

THURSDAY

FRIDAY

SATURDAY

I am **ABUNDANT.**

Today I am grateful for:

SUNDAY

MONDAY

TUESDAY

WEDNESDAY

THURSDAY

FRIDAY

SATURDAY

I am **ACTIVE**.

Today I am grateful for:

SUNDAY

MONDAY

TUESDAY

WEDNESDAY

THURSDAY

FRIDAY

SATURDAY

I am **BEAUTIFUL.**

Today I am grateful for:

SUNDAY

MONDAY

TUESDAY

WEDNESDAY

THURSDAY

FRIDAY

SATURDAY

I am **BOLD.**

Today I am grateful for:

SUNDAY

MONDAY

TUESDAY

WEDNESDAY

THURSDAY

FRIDAY

SATURDAY

I am **CAPABLE.**

Today I am grateful for:

SUNDAY

MONDAY

TUESDAY

WEDNESDAY

THURSDAY

FRIDAY

SATURDAY

I am **CHEERFUL.**

Today I am grateful for:

SUNDAY

MONDAY

TUESDAY

WEDNESDAY

THURSDAY

FRIDAY

SATURDAY

I am **COMMITTED.**

Today I am grateful for:

SUNDAY

MONDAY

TUESDAY

WEDNESDAY

THURSDAY

FRIDAY

SATURDAY

I am COMPASSIONATE.

Today I am grateful for:

SUNDAY

MONDAY

TUESDAY

WEDNESDAY

THURSDAY

FRIDAY

SATURDAY

I am **CONFIDENT.**

Today I am grateful for:

SUNDAY

MONDAY

TUESDAY

WEDNESDAY

THURSDAY

FRIDAY

SATURDAY

I am **CONSISTENT.**

Today I am grateful for:

SUNDAY

MONDAY

TUESDAY

WEDNESDAY

THURSDAY

FRIDAY

SATURDAY

I am **COURAGEOUS.**

Today I am grateful for:

SUNDAY

MONDAY

TUESDAY

WEDNESDAY

THURSDAY

FRIDAY

SATURDAY

I am **CREATIVE.**

Today I am grateful for:

SUNDAY

MONDAY

TUESDAY

WEDNESDAY

THURSDAY

FRIDAY

SATURDAY

I am **DETERMINED.**

Today I am grateful for:

SUNDAY

MONDAY

TUESDAY

WEDNESDAY

THURSDAY

FRIDAY

SATURDAY

I am **DISCIPLINED.**

Today I am grateful for:

SUNDAY

MONDAY

TUESDAY

WEDNESDAY

THURSDAY

FRIDAY

SATURDAY

I am **EMPOWERED.**

Today I am grateful for:

SUNDAY

MONDAY

TUESDAY

WEDNESDAY

THURSDAY

FRIDAY

SATURDAY

I am **ENOUGH**.

Today I am grateful for:

SUNDAY

MONDAY

TUESDAY

WEDNESDAY

THURSDAY

FRIDAY

SATURDAY

I am **EXCITING**.

Today I am grateful for:

SUNDAY

MONDAY

TUESDAY

WEDNESDAY

THURSDAY

FRIDAY

SATURDAY

I am **FAITHFUL**.

Today I am grateful for:

SUNDAY

MONDAY

TUESDAY

WEDNESDAY

THURSDAY

FRIDAY

SATURDAY

I am **FEARLESS**.

Today I am grateful for:

SUNDAY

MONDAY

TUESDAY

WEDNESDAY

THURSDAY

FRIDAY

SATURDAY

I am **FOCUSED**.

Today I am grateful for:

SUNDAY

MONDAY

TUESDAY

WEDNESDAY

THURSDAY

FRIDAY

SATURDAY

I am **FORGIVING.**

Today I am grateful for:

SUNDAY

MONDAY

TUESDAY

WEDNESDAY

THURSDAY

FRIDAY

SATURDAY

I am **FRIENDLY**.

Today I am grateful for:

SUNDAY

MONDAY

TUESDAY

WEDNESDAY

THURSDAY

FRIDAY

SATURDAY

I am **HONEST**.

Today I am grateful for:

SUNDAY

MONDAY

TUESDAY

WEDNESDAY

THURSDAY

FRIDAY

SATURDAY

I am **INCREDIBLE.**

Today I am grateful for:

SUNDAY

_____

MONDAY

_____

TUESDAY

_____

WEDNESDAY

_____

THURSDAY

_____

FRIDAY

_____

SATURDAY

_____

I am **INDEPENDENT.**

Today I am grateful for:

SUNDAY

MONDAY

TUESDAY

WEDNESDAY

THURSDAY

FRIDAY

SATURDAY

I am **INNOVATIVE**.

Today I am grateful for:

SUNDAY

MONDAY

TUESDAY

WEDNESDAY

THURSDAY

FRIDAY

SATURDAY

I am **INSPIRED.**

Today I am grateful for:

SUNDAY

MONDAY

TUESDAY

WEDNESDAY

THURSDAY

FRIDAY

SATURDAY

I am **JOY.**

Today I am grateful for:

SUNDAY

MONDAY

TUESDAY

WEDNESDAY

THURSDAY

FRIDAY

SATURDAY

I am **KNOWLEDGEABLE.**

Today I am grateful for:

SUNDAY

MONDAY

TUESDAY

WEDNESDAY

THURSDAY

FRIDAY

SATURDAY

I am **LIMITLESS.**

Today I am grateful for:

SUNDAY

MONDAY

TUESDAY

WEDNESDAY

THURSDAY

FRIDAY

SATURDAY

I am **LOVING.**

Today I am grateful for:

SUNDAY

MONDAY

TUESDAY

WEDNESDAY

THURSDAY

FRIDAY

SATURDAY

I am **MOTIVATED.**

Today I am grateful for:

SUNDAY

MONDAY

TUESDAY

WEDNESDAY

THURSDAY

FRIDAY

SATURDAY

I am ORIGINAL.

Today I am grateful for:

SUNDAY

MONDAY

TUESDAY

WEDNESDAY

THURSDAY

FRIDAY

SATURDAY

I am **PATIENT**.

Today I am grateful for:

SUNDAY

MONDAY

TUESDAY

WEDNESDAY

THURSDAY

FRIDAY

SATURDAY

I am **PERSISTENT**.

Today I am grateful for:

SUNDAY

MONDAY

TUESDAY

WEDNESDAY

THURSDAY

FRIDAY

SATURDAY

I am **POSITIVE**.

Today I am grateful for:

SUNDAY

MONDAY

TUESDAY

WEDNESDAY

THURSDAY

FRIDAY

SATURDAY

I am **POWERFUL**.

Today I am grateful for:

SUNDAY

MONDAY

TUESDAY

WEDNESDAY

THURSDAY

FRIDAY

SATURDAY

I am **PRACTICAL**.

Today I am grateful for:

SUNDAY

MONDAY

TUESDAY

WEDNESDAY

THURSDAY

FRIDAY

SATURDAY

I am **READY**.

Today I am grateful for:

SUNDAY

MONDAY

TUESDAY

WEDNESDAY

THURSDAY

FRIDAY

SATURDAY

I am **REALISTIC**.

Today I am grateful for:

SUNDAY

MONDAY

TUESDAY

WEDNESDAY

THURSDAY

FRIDAY

SATURDAY

I am **RELENTLESS**.

Today I am grateful for:

SUNDAY

MONDAY

TUESDAY

WEDNESDAY

THURSDAY

FRIDAY

SATURDAY

I am **RELIABLE**.

Today I am grateful for:

SUNDAY

MONDAY

TUESDAY

WEDNESDAY

THURSDAY

FRIDAY

SATURDAY

I am **RESOURCEFUL**.

Today I am grateful for:

SUNDAY

MONDAY

TUESDAY

WEDNESDAY

THURSDAY

FRIDAY

SATURDAY

I am **RESPONSIBLE**.

Today I am grateful for:

SUNDAY

MONDAY

TUESDAY

WEDNESDAY

THURSDAY

FRIDAY

SATURDAY

I am **RICH**.

Today I am grateful for:

SUNDAY

MONDAY

TUESDAY

WEDNESDAY

THURSDAY

FRIDAY

SATURDAY

I am **STRONG**.

Today I am grateful for:

SUNDAY

MONDAY

TUESDAY

WEDNESDAY

THURSDAY

FRIDAY

SATURDAY

I am **SUCCESSFUL**.

Today I am grateful for:

SUNDAY

MONDAY

TUESDAY

WEDNESDAY

THURSDAY

FRIDAY

SATURDAY

I am **THOUGHTFUL**.

Today I am grateful for:

SUNDAY

_____

MONDAY

_____

TUESDAY

_____

WEDNESDAY

_____

THURSDAY

_____

FRIDAY

_____

SATURDAY

_____

I am **UNIQUE**.

Today I am grateful for:

SUNDAY

MONDAY

TUESDAY

WEDNESDAY

THURSDAY

FRIDAY

SATURDAY

I am **UNSTOPPABLE**.

Today I am grateful for:

SUNDAY

MONDAY

TUESDAY

WEDNESDAY

THURSDAY

FRIDAY

SATURDAY

I believe.

Today I am grateful for:

SUNDAY

MONDAY

TUESDAY

WEDNESDAY

THURSDAY

FRIDAY

SATURDAY

I AM.

ABOUT THE AUTHOR

Elaine's mission is to EMPOWER others to use their gifts and talents to rise and soar.

For the past 10 years, Elaine has been running her photography business in the Lehigh Valley (Pennsylvania) and surrounding areas. She has mastered the "perfect headshot" and has enjoyed photographing thousands of people all over the country. She has been published in multiple magazines and has worked on numerous film projects and commercials.

She has expanded and now offers classes in photography, branding and social media, and runs motivational mastermind classes on-line and in person.

Known as a serial entrepreneur, she has multiple side hustles and loves art! She's a mom, a teacher, a photographer, brand strategist, wife, team leader, author, DIY'er, speaker and lover of life!!

She lives in Easton, PA with her filmmaker husband, Zeke, and three daughters, Julia, Emily & Kate.

www.elainezelker.com

Made in the USA
Columbia, SC
24 December 2019